Lord Coleridge

The History of the Town of Ottery S. Mary

A Lecture Delivered at the Church Institute in September, 1897

Lord Coleridge

The History of the Town of Ottery S. Mary
A Lecture Delivered at the Church Institute in September, 1897

ISBN/EAN: 9783337007652

Printed in Europe, USA, Canada, Australia, Japan

Cover: Foto ©ninafisch / pixelio.de

More available books at **www.hansebooks.com**

THE
HISTORY OF THE TOWN
OF
OTTERY S. MARY.

A LECTURE DELIVERED AT THE CHURCH

INSTITUTE, IN SEPTEMBER, 1897,

BY

'LONDON :

HUTCHINGS AND CROWSLEY, PRINTERS, 123 FULHAM ROAD,

S.W.

At the request of my friends I set out this lecture exactly as I delivered it.

I only wish it were a more worthy expression of the love which I bear towards the home of my birth.

COLERIDGE.

Heath's Court,
  Ottery S. Mary.

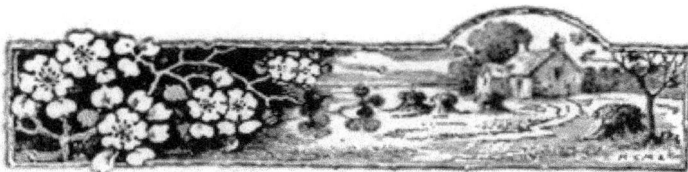

THE HISTORY OF THE TOWN

OF

OTTERY S. MARY.

⟨ornament⟩

THE history of our Church having been already described to you by Mr. Dickinson, with so much charming learning, I have chosen as my subject the History of our Town.

A friend of mine said to me the other day, " You surely do not seriously mean to give a lecture on the History of our Town ?" " Why not ?" said I. " Because," said he, " our Town has no history !"

Wait a bit, my friend. To every town of any antiquity there is a history. Though men, as individuals, be born and die, yet, collectively, each town is a small fragment of enduring humanity.

It is a mirror, wherein are reflected the manners and the customs, the joys and the sorrows, the charities and the tyrannies, the loves and the hatreds, of each succeeding age. And although our town may not have stood sieges, or crowned kings, in the simple tenor of its simple life we have a history, interesting enough to him who loves it.

Our town then—our dear old town—in which most of us were born, in which most of us will pass away, how came it here, who lived here, what happened here, in a word, what is its history ?

On the hills which surround us lie the tombs of an extinct race, those barrows which still remain.

"The grassy barrows of the happier dead,"
sometimes bare, sometimes crowned with an appropriate group of pines.

The men who sleep under them looked down upon this broad vale, then clothed with the thick forest which grew over all the richer and less elevated soils. Clearings were gradually made as the tools men worked with became more efficient, and certain spots, favoured by Nature, became the settlements of increasing population. Such a spot was the site of Ottery S. Mary. Favoured indeed by Nature, and as one old writer quaintly puts it—

"On a sweet wholsom advanc'd ground,"
for the Teap Stream, which runs through the town, and has lately been closed in, ran down a lateral valley and joined the Otter, the " wild streamlet of the West," and the whole site was one

"looking to the West and fed
with honeyed rain and delicate air."

More than 800 years ago they came. They cleared the forest, tilled the lands, which consisted of what Gilbert White describes as " a warm, forward, crumbling loam," and the tracks, by which they went to their fields, remain in the meandering lanes through which we stroll to-day. They ground their corn in the town mill, and in the time of Edward the Confessor, more than 800 years ago, they dammed the river at Head Weir, and took its waters along the mill stream as we see it flowing.

When the Normans came I doubt not that the inhabitants were all tenants of one Lord of the Manor, forbidden to quit their native home, and compelled one and all to grind their corn at the Lords mill. Personally I should not object to the revival of this antient custom !

In the year 1061 the bounds of the Manor and Parish were fixed by Edward the Confessor, who granted the Manor to the Chapter of the Cathedral at Rouen in Normandy at a rental of 66 marks. Thus early was the prosperity of the town hindered and checked by absentee landlordism. For much of the wealth produced by the inhabitants went to feed the monks at Rouen, as in our day it goes to support the clerics of St. George's at Windsor.

Doubtless from earliest days our forefathers worshipped in some church, and probably on the site of the present building. All trace of such an early structure has passed away.

This much we know. In the year 1260, Bronscombe, Bishop of Exeter, consecrated a church here, how much remains of which has already been described to you by Mr. Dickinson in his lecture on the Church.

Down to the year 1337 men were born, lived, and died in this peaceful sleepy hollow, for the most part undisturbed by the rise and fall of Kings, or the drums and tramplings of foreign, or of civil wars.

But in the year 1337 a new era began in the history of our town. For in that year John de Grandisson, Bishop of Exeter, to whose pious memory every true Ottregian should bare his head, having purchased the Manor from the Chapter of Rouen, laid the foundations of the College, and proceeded to amplify, if not rebuild our Church. From 1337 until 1545, a period of 200 years, the town of Ottery S. Mary enjoyed a prosperity to which it has since been a stranger. Down to the year 1337 she had seen much of the rents produced by the tillers of the soil annually drawn away by France, and she, as I said, suffered from the evils of absentee landlordism. But from 1337 until 1545, she became an absentee landlord herself.

To the College was granted the Manor with its emoluments and rents, and revenues flowed in from London, Northam, Ipplepen, Ilsington, Ford, Chilsworthy, and Wysford Rivers. The College consisted of 40 members, Warden, Precentor, Minister, Sacristan, Priests, Clerks, Choir-boys, and a Master of Grammar.

Let us in fancy pay a visit to our town during this flourishing period.

On the hill overlooking the inhabitants stood the great Collegiate Church, dedicated to the Blessed Virgin Mary and to Edward the Confessor. In outward form it differed little from its aspect now, save that the Dorset aisle had not then been built, the roof of the nave and chancel was some few feet higher than now, and I doubt not that a spire stood upon each tower. The windows were filled with glorious stained glass, rich and dark in colour, filled with armorial bearings of the founder and his relatives, and plunging the interior into mysterious gloom. Various altars and rood screens met the eye, and the walls and roof were glowing with colour.

Pass outside. To the south of the South Tower, and adjoining it, stood the Chapter House, and along the wall bordering on what we still call the college, where flourishes the avenue of pollard elms, ran the cloisters, probably of wood, and forming a solemn walk for pious meditation. The entrance to the churchyard still remains, facing down the street, but no steps were there, the entrance being on the flat, and over the entrance stood a noble gate-way, which was afterwards turned into a house which was standing early in the present century. On the eastern side of the gateway there was a stile, giving in to the churchyard, from whence on the other side ran the church path in later times to Cadhay House.

At the entrance to the college stood an arched stone gateway covering a massive pair of gates, closed at night, forming the eastern limit of the sacred precincts of the college. Pass through these gates. What a noble vista! On the left stretched a long line of monastic buildings, storied windows, lofty and delicately carved gables, deep shadowy doorways. The present back door of the Manor House stood in one of these, and on one of its great iron stays you may see the same design as at Sand, in Sidbury, Knightstone, and other places. These buildings stood in one continuous line to the Warden House, round the corner, and as far as where the Manor House now stands. Along the south churchyard wall the cloisters ran. Within the college gateway and upon the south first came the "clink," or antient guardhouse, where malefactors were detained. A shed there still bears the name. Then came the various domestic buildings. The present Vicarage contains walls belonging to the Minister's house. A fragment of the Warden's house still stands where the Warden of the College lived. It was a stately building, thrusting forth two lateral wings towards the south, and hanging gardens dropped towards Hinde Street.

Right royal was the hospitality here displayed. Before a noble carved fire-place, still to be seen at the Vicarage, once hung the Warden's spits. At Heath's Court, so called from the family of the Heaths, which gave a Judge to the English Bench, stood the house of the Precentor, called the Chanter's House. The square block of Heath's Court fronting the garden consists of the walls of the Chanter's House, and we still reverently preserve in our Porch the painted oak beams which, from the roof, looked down upon the Precentor, and listened to the holy chanting of the Quire. Between the Chanter's House and the Manor House stood the house of the Sacristan. On the site of the present Manor House stood the Manor Hall, where Courts were held, and tenants came to do suit and service to their Lord, the College. Great oak beams supported the arched roof, and it was much the size of the present Town Hall. Sloping down from the Manor Hall, towards the Holcombe Brook, stood all the outhouses belonging to the College.

It was a goodly pile of buildings this, which covered the " sweet wholsom advanc'd ground."

ALEXANDER BARCLAY.

From the seclusion of these cloistered haunts came forth, in 1509, one of the great books of the English language. It was the work of Alexander Barclay, a Scotchman, who had been appointed Chaplain to the College by his friend the Warden—Bishop Cornish, Suffragan Bishop of Bath and Wells. It purports to be a translation of Sebastian Brandt's "¡Stultifera Navis," or " Ship of Fools," which fifteen years before had appeared in Germany written in the Swabian dialect, and had obtained wide fame in Europe. Barclay's work is a paraphrase rather than a translation. It contains much original work, and is thoroughly English in its character and allusions. In this allegory he finds a whipping-post whereat to lash the vices and follies of man. Let us ship off all fools to their native land. The ship, it is true, is almost sinking under its burden, but still he will find room on deck for his neighbours the secondaries at the College. The ship must not start without them! Standing midway in the blank space between Chaucer and Spenser, the writings of Barclay have an historical value apart from their literary merit. It is curious how many of our commonest sayings find their origin in his writings. When we say, "Man proposes, God disposes," "skin deep," "robbing Peter to pay Paul," "of two evils choose the least," "sticking like burrs," "over head and ears," "from pillar to post," "you cannot touch pitch and not be defiled," "making the mouth water," "out of sight out of mind," "the burnt child dreads the fire," we are unconsciously using phrases which appear in their first form in Barclay's writings.

While the Canons could pray they could feast also right royally.

Hither came Henry VI. in 1451, and was entertained sumptuously for two nights at the College. The next royal visitor was Henry VII., who came in 1497, at the termination of the insurrection of Perkin Warbeck.

Let us take a stroll through the town. It did not then present the somewhat mean aspect which I am sorry to say most of our streets exhibit. This is due partly to the destructive fires which took place in July, 1604, on March 16, 1767, and on May 25, 1866, partly to the total lack of artistic feeling which seems to characterise the more modern buildings of the West. You have only to visit Kent, Surrey, Sussex, or Hampshire, to mark the difference.

Beautiful stone-mullioned windows met the eye at every turn : At the head of Jesu Street, now Yonder Street, there was a chapel, dedicated to St. Budeaux, from whence we get the name "Butts Hill." It was a sweet old custom to invite the wayfarer on entering the town to stop, for however short a time, to pray. Hard by the chapel, close to "the Shutts," stood the great Poarth House, which was standing in 1747, every stone of which is gone.

In Mill Street, partly on the site of the present Ralegh House, stood the house, "be-turreted, and wearing a monasterial aspect," which the great Sir Walter Ralegh, who was born at Poer's Hayes, now Hayesbarton, for a time inhabited. Ralegh's father occupied Poer's Hayes as a tenant of the great Duke family. In after years, Ralegh, when a powerful man at the Court of Queen Elizabeth, wished for the love of his birthplace to buy the estate. The Mr. Duke of the day, wishing neither to sell the estate nor to offend Sir Walter Ralegh, replied that it was such an honour to be Sir Walter's landlord that he could not find it in his heart to bring the connection to a close, and so the incident ended. The only relic of the house in Mill Street which Ralegh occupied is the carved head which you may see over the front door of the present Ralegh House.

SIR WALTER RALEGH.

Beyond the Town Mill, which stood on a Mill green, there were other mills, leather and tucking mills, and afterwards fulling mills, and beyond again, a chapel of St. Saviour, which gave its name to St. Saviour's Bridge, then a stone arched bridge, containing in the depths of one of its piers a small altar, with sacred flame alight, and not the useful, but hideous, structure which now spans the stream. This is the supplanter of an old stone bridge which was washed away December 7, 1849. Would that another such flood would come !

In the neighbourhood at Holcombe stood a stately house, of the beautiful architecture of the Middle Ages, within the precincts of which was enshrined a chapel dedicated to St. Leonard. Not one stone of this old house remains. Rude hands, in the memory of persons still alive, destroyed the last relics of this antient seat, and the occupier now lives in a square box, with mean roof, in the " packing case " style of architecture, with square holes cut in the walls for windows. I hope he is comfortable ! Some fine old woodwork, the only salvage from the wreck, may yet be seen in the prayer-room at the Manor House. This building is only too typical of the decay of art in the West of England. Knightstone was once the possession of the stately race of Bonville, and it is to Cecily Bonville, first Marchioness of Dorset, and afterwards Marchioness of Stafford, that we owe the beautiful addition to our Church of the Dorset aisle, a facsimile of the roof of which is seen in a similar addition to the Church at Collumpton. On the attainder of her son, Henry Grey, Duke of Suffolk, Knightstone passed to the Crown, and was bought by a member of the Sherman family. In 1567 Gideon Sherman, a merchant of Ottery S. Mary, built the house as now we see it, with its modest, yet dignified, elevation, its ample and well-proportioned hall. Mr. Matthew Ellis may well be congratulated on the possession of so picturesque and interesting a home. May the fate of Holcombe never overtake it ! John Haydon lived at Cadhay, and there he built the lordly quadrangular house which by its beauty preserves still green the memory of him who bid it rise from the level meadows bordering on the stream.

The Haydons of England are extinct ; but they are a numerous and flourishing colony in America. Not long ago they deputed one of their family to come over and collect information about their ancestors. It was from Woodbury that the Devon branch of the family sprang, in which church you may still see the great slabs of tombstones which once covered their remains. The sacrilegious hands, however, of the restorers have, for the sake of putting down some paltry tiles, removed their tombstones from the remains they cover. On them you may read : " Here lies the body of John Haydon," &c. The body does not lie there. The people who do such things have been described for all time by Charles Lamb as " those sapient trouble-tombs ! "

The College was dissolved by Henry VIII., and the Corporation and the King's School took possession of the antient buildings. The Manor, granted to the Earl of

Hertford, afterwards the Protector Somerset, reverted to the Crown on his execution for high treason, in 1552, and was afterwards sold by Charles I. The great tithes on which the College flourished found their way to the Dean and Chapter of Windsor. It is noteworthy that on the restoration of the Church in 1849 no farthing towards the expence was contributed by that august and reverend body.

With the dissolution of the College most of the glory of our town departed. The great buildings of Grandisson fell gradually into decay, and a severe Protestantism removed all marks of the Roman Catholic religion in and about the Church and elsewhere.

On the death of Henry VIII. the Protector Somerset ruled the land in the minority of the young king, Edward VI. Somerset was penetrated with reforming zeal. Much that he did was the fruit of sincere sympathy with the poor. He encouraged husbandry and tillage, "the Paunch," as was said, "of the Commonwealth." But he fell into the mistake of believing that the poorer people could happily be made to work by law, and that they were all as fervid Protestants as himself. Away went the rood-skreens and images from the Church, on which the pious gaze of generations had been fixed. Away went the Mass in Latin, and in came the Liturgy in English.

The faiths of men cannot be changed by law. In 1549 an insurrection against the new policy arose in the West. Exeter was besieged by the Roman Catholics, and Mohun's Ottery, four miles from Honiton, of which a stately gateway yet remains, became the gathering ground of the Protestant forces, which were ultimately to subdue the rising.

At Mohun's Ottery lived Sir Peter Carew, a noble member of a generous race. Gathering his forces together he, with his uncle, Sir Gawen Carew, of Wood, in Kentisbeare, Lord Russell, and others, marched on Exeter to raise the siege. A bloody skirmish was fought at Fenny Bridges, and the slain are said to have numbered 600 men.

Under the floor of the North Vestry lie six feet of human bones. They are the bones of bodies that must have been flung there in a heap. It is believed that the bones of the slaughtered soldiers have found in that sacred spot their last resting-place. Let us hope that they have found in death that unity of spirit which must always exist between men who hold their faiths so keenly that they are ready to die for them.

Our vale and river were not unnoticed by poets. William Browne, the author of Britannia's Pastorals, who lived some time in Ottery S. Mary, and who is said, on the authority of Southey, to have written the two fine inscriptions in the small South Chapel ; one on John Sherman and his son, who died on the same day, in 1617, and one on the wife of Gideon Sherman, who died in the first week of her marriage, speaks of

> " The nymphs by Tamar, Tavy, Exe, and Taw,
> By Torridge, Otter, Ock, by Dort and Plym,
> With all the Nayades that fish and swim
> In their cleare streams."

His poetry is full of loving descriptions of natural scenery, though at times overloaded with conceits.

Sometimes, however, he rises to a lofty strain. Thus, invoking Metanoia, or Repentance, he sings :—

> Vain man, doe not mistrust
>   Of Heaven winning,
> Nor, though the most unjust,
>   Despaire for sinning,
> God will be seen his sentence changing,
> If He behold thee wicked ways estranging.
>
> Climbe up where pleasures dwell
>   In flowery allies,
> And taste the living well
>   That decks the vallies,
> Faire Metanoia is attending,
> To crowne thee with those joys which know no
>   ending.

The parish Register contains an entry of the burial of " William Browne," on December 1, 1645.

Michael Drayton, who died in 1631, in his Polyolbion, that great poem hymning the streams of England, comes to our valley. Its broad pastoral character strikes his eye, for he says :—

> Here I'll unyoke awhile, and turn my steeds to meat,
> The lane grows large and wide, my team begins to sweat.

I will now pass over a hundred years and come to the time of the Great Civil War. England was divided into two armed camps. On the one side fought those who upheld " the right Divine of Kings to govern wrong," on the other, those who maintained the right of Parliament to

govern the Commonwealth to be supreme. The horror of
that time no words can bring before you. Father fought
against son, and brother against brother. Even our parish
clerk in the general overturn forsook his duties and ceased
to make entries of births, deaths, and marriages, in our
Parish Register.

Our town became the quarters of the King's troops.
They withdrew, however, further west beyond Exe, on the
advance of the Parliamentary army. Hither came on

SIR THOMAS FAIRFAX.

October 29, 1645, the Commander-in-Chief, Sir Thomas Fairfax, accompanied by Ireton as Commissary, and John Pickering as Colonel, to join the forces of the Commonwealth which were already quartered in the town.

Fairfax stayed from October 29—December 6, at the Chanter's House, the house in which I live, and in our dining room, then called the Great Parlour, he met the Lord General Cromwell, and it is said, determined on the plan of campaign

OLIVER CROMWELL.

against the King's forces in the West, which culminated in the capitulation on honourable terms of Sir Ralph Hopton in Cornwall in the following March. Here also a graceful ceremony was performed. A number of members of Parliament, in the name of both Houses, presented Fairfax with a fair Jewel, set with diamonds of great value, which they tied with blue ribbon and hung about his neck, in grateful recognition of his signal services at the battle of Naseby.

One day a trumpeter came from Prince Charles, afterwards Charles II., upon a design of a mediation of peace, whom Fairfax referred to his masters the Parliament. It is said that Cromwell issued a requisition to the inhabitants to supply him with arms and money, which they refused to do.

Sickness overtook the army during its stay. They died at the rate of seven, eight and nine a day for several weeks together of the new disease, akin to the plague, which broke out and which necessitated their removal to Tiverton on December 6. Colonel Pickering, who had fought at Naseby, had been present at the storming of Bridgewater, who had been the first within the enemy's works at the capture of Bristol, described as "an active pious gentleman, who lived so much to God and his country," fell a victim. It is said, though I do not vouch for the accuracy of the fact, that he lies in full armour under the floor of the Church in the middle aisle of the nave.

Forty years roll by and we come to 1685. That was the year of the rebellion of the Duke of Monmouth, which had its source in the undisguised attempt of James II. to force the religion of the Roman Catholics upon the Protestants of England.

Sir Walter Yonge, of the Great House, Colyton, was then building his house at Escot, of which the antient stone pillars at Fairmile, which marked the beginning of the avenue which led to the house, alone remain. Built from the designs of Inigo Jones, one of England's greatest architects, it was burnt to the ground in 1808. John Locke, the philosopher, a friend of Sir Walter Yonge, is said to have stayed there and to have planted some of the beeches which still stand in the park, notably the Horse-shoe clump.

Sir Walter Yonge was known to be a sympathiser with the Monmouth party, though discreetly absent from the spot, and his workmen building his house threw down their tools, shouldered pikes and staves, and joined the rebel army at Sedgemoor, near Bridgewater. The slaughter of the poor half armed peasants was pitiful. Some, taken alive, were tried before Judge Jefferies. The Assizes which he held have always been called, and rightly called, the Bloody Assizes. With a view of inspiring terror the poor prisoners were sent to be executed in the neighbourhood from which they came, and to warn Sir Walter Yonge and others, some were executed at Bittery Cross, not far from Talaton, and, tradition says, at

Spence Cross too.   They probably were buried where they hung, silently, and with the burial of a dog, or else hung in chains till the flesh rotted off the grinning skeletons.

Poor souls! had they but waited! for in four years time the king against whose tyrannies they rose, was an exile in a foreign land.   In 1688, favoured by a " Protestant wind," as the wind from the North-East was ever afterwards called, William III., on whom the hopes of the friends of religious and political freedom were fixed, landed in Torbay and, after resting at Ford House, near Newton Abbot, and Exeter, dined in our town on November 21, on the way to Honiton, and James II. fled the country, happily never to return.

By this time another public building had been added to the town.   In this street stands one of the oldest Nonconformist places of worship in the Kingdom.   It was built on the site of an old bowling green where our forefathers practised that antient West country game.   "Stay," said Sir Francis Drake, when the news of the advent in sight of the Spanish Armada came to him as he was bowling on the Hoe at Plymouth, "Stay, and let us first finish the game!" Built of bricks in the style known as "the Flemish bond," o'erhued with rich colours from the palette of Time, it testifies to the austere yet deep-seated piety of the men who raised it.   To my eye the existence of this simple and old-world house of prayer is both historically and artistically a charming feature of our town.   Round it sleep the members of its congregation.   May the quiet graveyard never be disturbed.

Time was when, if more than five people beyond a family met to worship there, or elsewhere, in any other manner than was allowed by the practice of the Church of England, the worshippers were criminals, liable, if they persisted, to be sentenced by a single magistrate to transportation, deprived of the right of trial by jury, on the evidence of spies and informers.   Tradition says there once existed a trap door in the floor, at the back of the pulpit, through which the minister could bolt, in case of danger, into the vaults below, which still exist below the present schoolroom.   This old pulpit, a fair oaken structure, was, within our time, taken away and destroyed to make room for the present organ ; an act of barbarism strongly and justly resented at the time.   Those who wantonly break these links with the past, are guilty of that which nothing can repair or justify.

I am afraid that the charity and good feeling of our townsfolk were not sufficient to make the use of this means of escape unnecessary, as the following story will show:—

In the time of Charles I., a Mr. Pynsent held two benefices, one in Cornwall and one at Talaton. How he managed to attend to them both may excite our pardonable curiosity. But he was ejected from his living in Cornwall for gross immorality. No one, however, complaining against him at Talaton, he continued there to minister to souls. When Cromwell became the Lord Protector of the Commonwealth he proceeded to purge the church by the casting out of scandalous ministers, and we do not wonder that Mr. Pynsent was removed and the living sequestrated. The cure was given to a Mr. Sprat, the father of the Bishop of Rochester, and on his death to Mr. Robert Collins. This Mr. Robert Collins was an Ottery man and a man of substance. He lived in the Chanter's House, now Heath's Court. His ministrations at Talaton were somewhat disturbed by Mr. Pynsent. Mr. Pynsent, though he had to leave the parsonage at Talaton, continued to live in the parish. He swore that he would never go to church till the church was restored to him. He regularly attended Divine service however— outside—peeping through the windows, which must have been somewhat disturbing to the congregation and to the pulpit eloquence of Mr. Collins !

On the restoration of Charles II., Mr. Pynsent, scandalous minister though he was, was promptly restored to his benefice, and Mr. Collins as promptly ejected. But, alas for his oath that he would never enter the church till he was restored to the living, for on the day of his restoration he was smitten with paralysis, and never entered the church again until he was carried thither four years later to be buried. We need not wonder at the people regarding his calamity as the just visitation of an offended God.

But we have not done with Mr. Collins. The Act of Uniformity, passed in 1662, declared that every minister should declare his assent and consent to everything contained in the Book of Common Prayer, on pain of being *ipso facto* deprived of his benefice. It was owing to Mr. Collins being unable, for conscience sake, to subscribe his assent, that he, with 2000 other ministers, was ejected, and became in the eye of the law a Nonconformist. He likewise disregarded the Conventicle Act, passed in 1664, of which I have already spoken.

So on Sept. 25, 1670, the churchwardens and constables, with a great mob after them, beset the Chanter's House upon an information that some schoolboys had given, that a meeting had been kept there. They declared " that he might be as godly as he would on week-days, but that he should not be so godly on Sundays." Sir Peter Prideaux, of Netherton Hall, issued a warrant to break open the doors of the Chanter's House and secure the person of Mr. Collins and others, and bring them before him, which was done. Sir Peter courteously assured him that he was the minister of the devil ! A descent was made upon his property to answer for the fine levied.

No persecution could break down the resolve of Mr. Collins to pray to God in his house, if he chose, with his friends and neighbours.

On August 20. 1675, there being no service or sermon in the Parish Church, many of the leading inhabitants of Ottery S. Mary desired Mr. Collins to preach there. He refused to do that, but preached in his own house, and people thronged to hear him both in the forenoon and afternoon. A prosecution followed.

Mr. Collins was convicted and fined, so was Mr. Warwick Ledgingham, the Lord of the Manor, and in particular Mr. Farrington, for knowing of the meeting, but not discovering it !

On August 20, 1679, Mr. Haydon, of Cadhay, broke open his gates and doors and made a strict search. Nobody was there but his household. But upon discovery afterwards that twenty-three persons had been there, they were all indicted at the sessions for an unlawful assembly.

On May 15, 1681, Mr. Haydon, with several officers, demanded admission, which being denied, they broke open the great gate and then the doors. But they only found three persons there beside the family, and five being necessary to constitute the offence of attending a meeting, Mr. Haydon was foiled

But not for long. For ten days afterwards he arrested Mr. Collins as he was on horseback attending a funeral. He shut him up and proceeded to demand that he should take the Corporation Oath, and on refusal he imprisoned him for six months. He employed his time when in jail in preaching and praying with the criminals, especially with one poor wretch under sentence of death.

The magistrates repeatedly convicted him of the offence of not going to church, while the ecclesiastical courts excommunicated him, which made it illegal for him to do so !

He was also convicted of the offence of living in his home, it being within five miles of the place where he had been minister.

At last this constant persecution broke him down. In 1685 he sold the Chanter's House to Mr Thomas Heath, and withdrew with his family to Holland, where he died, brave and unflinching to the last. His last act was to bequeath a sum of money (£20) to the building of the meeting-house. Such men deserve to be remembered.

Near St. Saviour's Bridge you may see a dignified and substantial building now divided into separate dwellings. This was the Parish Workhouse, erected in 1738. It was built to hold 200 inmates when crowded. I have spoken to persons who remember chained lunatics inhabiting the ground-floor rooms, to whom passers-by would toss bones and scraps through the open window, which were eagerly seized and devoured by the poor raving creatures, to whom, in those days, little compassion was shown. It was not until 1838 that the Parish Workhouse was closed on the opening of the Union Workhouse at Honiton.

In the year 1760 came the Rev. John Coleridge from the Grammar School at South Molton to be schoolmaster at the King's School. He was a profound mathematician, a learned divine, and a correct and ardent scholar, and from the present oak pulpit, the work of an Ottery carpenter, he used to declaim to the gaping congregation quotations from the Bible in Hebrew, they being always taken by the worshippers as the very words of the Holy Ghost. He brought with him, as a scholar, Francis Buller, who subsequently sat for twenty-two years as a Judge of the High Court, and was one of the ablest of his brethren. In those days it was generally supposed that a man might legally chastise his wife, provided that the stick which he used was thin enough to go through the wedding ring. But Judge Buller was said, I believe erroneously said, to have laid down the law that the stick might be as thick as his thumb. Great curiosity was exhibited on the part of husbands to know how thick that was. Alas ! modern civilization has long taken away this privilege from the unhappy husbands of shrewish wives !

SAMUEL TAYLOR COLERIDGE.

Here, in 1772, was born the poet, Samuel Taylor Coleridge. As a boy he rambled on the banks of the Otter, and has expressed his love for it in the well-known sonnet—

Dear native Brook ! wild streamlet of the West,
How many various fated years have passed ;
What blissful, and what anguish hours, since last
I skimmed the smooth, thin stone along thy breast,
Numbering its light leaps ! Yet so deep impressed
Sink the sweet scenes of childhood, that mine eyes
I never shut amid the sunny blaze ;
But straight with all their tints thy waters rise ;
Thy crossing plank, thy marge with willows grey,
And bedded sand that, veined with various dyes,
Gleamed through thy bright transparence. On my way
Visions of childhood ! oft have ye beguiled
Lone manhood's cares, yet waking fondest sighs.
Ah ! that I once more were a careless child !

In the year 1789 he cut his initials in the rock at Pixie's Parlour, whither he would roam by himself, and muse on the peaceful beauty of the scene, picturing to himself the Pixies dancing their antics around.

" Then with quaint music hymn the parting gleam,
   By lonely Otter's sleep persuading stream ;
   Or where his wave, with loud unquiet song,
   Dashed o'er the rocky channel, froths along ;
   Or where his silver waters smoothed to rest, -
   The tall tree's shadow sleeps upon his breast."

Going from Ottery up to Christ's Hospital, London, he there met Charles Lamb, prince of English essayists. To Charles Lamb he must have spoken of the melody of our church bells haunting his ears, for although Charles Lamb never came to our Town, and never heard the bells, yet in one of the plays which he wrote, he makes his characters allude to them thus :—

Marg. : Hark the bells, John !

John : Those are the church bells of S. Mary Ottery.

Marg.: I know it.

John : S. Mary Ottery, my native village,
     In the sweet shire of Devon.
     Those are the bells.

In this passage we seem to hear the boy Samuel Taylor Coleridge, in the midst of the smoke and din of the London streets, with his imagination slipping back to the sights and sounds of his childhood, pouring forth his recollections to his boy friend, Charles Lamb.

Nor could Thomas Hood prevent himself from punning on the name of our town, for we read in his " Angler's Farewell " the following libel on our river : —

     Oh ! there is not a one-pound prize,
     To be got in this fresh-water lottery ;
       What then, can I deem
       Of so fishless a stream,
     But that 'tis—like St. Mary's—" *Ottery.*"

The year 1790 saw a great impetus given to the serge trade of the town by the erection of the factory. It was built by Sir George Yonge at a cost of £40,000, and in the field below Cadhay you may yet see the place whence the bricks were dug. It contained at that time, I believe, the largest water wheel in the kingdom, and to this day its size, I am told, is only exceeded by the Forster's wheel on the Wharf at Bradford. Bishop Selwyn, of New Zealand, and afterwards of Lichfield, coming here in 1867, with his experience of the Black Country, held up his hands in amazement at the sight of a factory, with ivy climbing on it to the roof, and no smoke!

Escot saw a gay and festive sight on August 13, 1789, when George III. and the three Princesses visited Sir George Yonge, then Secretary of State for War, and were entertained by him right royally. We may be sure that our townsfolk were not behindhand in welcoming their Sovereign, who gloried as he said in the name of Briton, and who was the first king since the Revolution who was so regarded by the people. They had not then read the savage satire of Peter Pindar on his visit, at whose japes we still laugh.

We now come to the time when this country and France were at deadly war, and we catch a fleeting glimpse of the national hero Lord Nelson. After the battle of the Nile, when by the destruction of the French fleet the schemes of Buonaparte for the conquest of Great Britain were, for the time, frustrated, the nation, in a fit of generosity, thought of buying a country estate, and presenting it to Nelson, as was done in the case of the Duke of Marlborough. Hembury Fort House was suggested, and Nelson came down to inspect it. My grandfather well remembered seeing the great Admiral riding on horseback through the lanes by Buckerell. He lay at what was then the old Golden Lion Inn at Honiton, now partly turned into the Post Office.

There is a pretty story of him, which makes one understand the personal devotion which he inspired in his subordinates. While at Honiton he remembered that it was the home of Captain B. Westcott, who had served under him. He inquired whether any members of his family still lived there. On being told that an aunt, Miss Westcott, was alive, he sent for her. In course of conversation he asked whether the family had any medal, and being told that they had not, he took a medal from his breast and handed it to her. This pretious relic is still treasured as an heirloom in the family.

Those were the days when the whole country side was up to repel the threatened invasion. The British fleet swept the Channel. The duty of the British ships was to confine the French fleet within the harbour of Brest. Bernard Frederick Coleridge, a brother of my grandfather, set forth from Heath's Court as a middy, aged 12, to join H.M.S. "Impeteux." They fared hard in those days, owing to the scandalous peculations at the Admiralty, which Lord Cochrane, one of the most brilliant naval captains in our history, first member for Honiton, and afterwards for Westminster, in vain exposed from his place in Parliament. The little lad writes to say that the only water to drink is stinking, "of the colour of the bark of a pear tree, with plenty of little maggots and weavils in it," and as for the biscuit "it quite makes your throat cold in eating it, owing to the maggots, which are very cold when you eat them, like a calf's foot jelly or blancmange, being very fat indeed." He longs for a bit of cheese, "for the maggots do not taste well without a bit of cheese." The boys played marbles on the poop, and sometimes were called away to see a poor fellow-creature subjected to the awful floggings of those days, sometimes consisting—think of it !—of five dozen lashes !

The next year the boy was promoted to a frigate, the "Phœnix," then lying in Plymouth Harbour. On Dec. 10. 1805, in a fit of boyish exultation he ran up the rigging to the topmast, lost his footing, fell down on the deck, and was killed on the spot.

Many of you know a tall Scotch pine which grows on our terrace, right against our house. That tree was planted by the little middy on the eve of his departure from his beloved home, which he was to revisit no more. On his tomb in Antony Churchyard you may still read the pathetic and appropriate inscription,

" He fell, to rise again."

At the head of the Volunteers and Militia of this part was General Simcoe, of Wolford Lodge. He had commanded the Queen's Rangers in the American War, he had been 1791-1796 the first Governor of Canada, and was a fine specimen of the cultivated man of arms. His son, Frances Gwillim Simcoe, educated at the King's School, under the Rev. George Coleridge, following in his father's profession, fell in the breach at Badajoz, in 1812. Col. James Coleridge, of Heath's Court, was General Simcoe's aide-de-camp, whom old Reed used to describe as "the finest disciplyned man, sir, that ever entered the British army. Between you and me, sir, I believe he was as good as Napoleon."

From the summit of the Hilly Field in the grounds of Heath's Court you can see with a telescope Wolford Lodge. Every morning up went the Colonel with his field-glass, and if a towel was hung on a stick out of a certain window, it was a summons to go up at once to the General. The town would then gape for the possible news of the landing of Buonaparte. On Telegraph Hill stands the ruin of the hut in which dwelt the man who worked the semaphore, which, with whirling arms signalled messages to St. Cyres Hill, on the east, and to Haldon on the west. There was a camp on Woodbury Common, and in the House on Black Hill may still be seen the Officers' Mess Room, from which the whole country could be surveyed. In the field across the river by St. Saviour's Bridge, still called the Barrack Field, were erected the barracks for the soldiers, and for some time this peaceful place echoed to the sound of trumpets and drums, and presented the aspect of a garrison town.

In 1806 General Simcoe issued his valedictory address to the Yeomanry and Volunteer Force of the Western District, on being employed on a foreign station. In contrast with the arms of precision and long ranges of to-day, close hand-grips with the bayonet was then the advice of the military authorities.

"The Major-General therefore desires that the volunteer in the charge may be exercised to increase his pace by degrees, so as to arrive with rapidity at the distance of 300 yards without any disorder, and in perfect breath and readiness to grapple with any opponent. The closing with the enemy becomes the courage of the country, and is firmly supported by that activity in which the Englishman participates with the Southern nations, and that strength in which he equals those of the North. A combination of those qualities and a due exercise therein must ensure victory. To close with the enemy has been the foundation of all our superiority by sea and by land; it was the principle of Marlborough, and the practice of Wolfe."

Happily for the troops the plague which drove away the Puritan soldiers in 1645 did not again appear, and in 1814, with the capture of Paris by the Allies, and the banishment of Buonaparte to Elba, the camp was broken up.

I do not know whether extreme longevity is much to be desired. But Mrs. Oldridge, the present Mother of the Parish, cannot compete with Mrs. Heath, who died at Heath's Court, and was buried on June 30, 1785, at the age of 113. She was the widow of Staplehill Heath, he being her second husband, she having been previously Mrs.

Elizabeth Bartlett. She could well remember King William's visit 97 years before!

The faculties of our folk are, I believe, acute. But I doubt if we could any of us do what Mr. Beedell, of Ottery S. Mary, did in 1823. He wrote, with the naked eye, in the circumference of a common-sized pea, the Lord's Prayer, the Belief, and two verses of the Third Psalm, all without the least abbreviation, certainly an amazing display of the power of the human eye, so much so as to attract the attention of the public journals of the day.

W. M. THACKERAY.

In the year 1849 Thackeray published the novel "Pendennis." He lived as a youth at Larkbeare House, and the scene of many of the incidents is laid in our neighbourhood. Clavering St. Mary is Ottery S. Mary, Chatteris is Exeter, Baymouth is Sidmouth, and the River Brawl is the Otter. In the first edition, illustrated by his own hand, we can see a picture of the Cock Tower of our church.

We read of the little river running off noisily westward, of the fair background of sunshiny hills that stretch towards the sea, of the pattens clacking through the empty streets, of the schoolboys making a good cheerful noise, scuffling with their feet as tney march into church and up the organ-loft stair, and blowing their noses a good deal during the sermon, of the factory, of the single old pair of posters that earned a scanty livelihood by transporting the gentry round about to the county dinners (and have we not often seen Bowers and the blue-roan horse issuing from the King's Arms on a similar errand?), of the hollow tree in Escot Park in which the young lovers deposited their letters, and, above all of the great grey towers rising up in purple splendour, of which the sun illuminates the delicate carving, deepening the shadows of the huge buttresses, and gilding the glittering windows.

These and other things, full of local colour, are they not written in a book, which can be bought for a small sum, and which is within the reach of almost anyone who loves our town and who can read and enjoy?

Nor does our town lag behind in producing men of eminence in science. Here in 1806 was born Edward Davy. His father lived in the present Ralegh House. It occupies part of the site of the house in which Sir Walter Ralegh lived. The only stone left of the latter is the old carved head which is the keystone of the arch over the front doorway of the present building, which is an admirable specimen of the quiet, homely family dwelling, dating from the end of the last century, and was built by Edward Davy's father.

Edward Davy was looked on by his family as a visionary, for in 1836 he sketched out a " Plan of Telegraphic Communication, by which intelligence may be conveyed, with Precision, to Unlimited Distances, in an Instant of Time, Independent of Fog or Darkness."

At the beginning of 1837 he laid down a copper wire round the Inner Circle at the Regent's Park, in London, and made wonderful experiments with it, and in March, 1837, he took the first step to patent his invention, by what was called "entering a caveat," and he deposited with Mr. Aikin, Secretary of the Society of Arts, a sealed description of his invention, anticipating Cook and Wheatstone, who have gone forth to the world as the original inventors, by two months. In May, 1837, Cook and Wheatstone applied for a patent, against which Davy entered an opposition. The Solicitor-General, however, allowed the patent to pass on the ground that the two inventions were different. No doubt there were differences, but there were identities as well. In November, 1837, a working model of his invention was shown at the Belgrave Institution, and from December 29,

1837, to November 10, 1838, he exhibited his discovery in a room rented at Exeter Hall. If he had had funds at his disposal to perfect and push his discoveries his fame might now be world-wide. Unfortunately, for private reasons, at the critical moment, he was obliged to emigrate to Australia on April 13, 1839, leaving the field to his rivals, Cook and Wheatstone.

In 1840 the machines were sent down from London and stowed in Ralegh House, where they remained for years, and were finally broken up and sold for old metal on the removal of the family to the adjoining house, called Colby, after a former occupant. ˙ The Daniell Cells, huge things of three or four gallons capacity, and some other relics found quite lately in an adjoining field, whither they had been carried, have now been carefully preserved. Edward Davy had a successful career in Australia, and only died in 1884.

Many other worthies have been connected with our town within living memory.

George James Cornish, 1794-1849, who sang the praises of St. Mary's Tower, the School, the Pixie's Bower, and the Maiden Pool, wherein the boys used to bathe, which was in the bend below Gosford Bridge before the course of the river was straightened ; Henry Nelson Coleridge, 1798-1843, brilliant scholar and man ˙of letters ; Richard Hurrell Froude, 1803-1836, a leader of Oxford thought ; William Hart Coleridge, 1789-1849, first Bishop of Barbadoes, who, is said, acting as Curate, to have christened Benjamin Disraeli, then a young man, St. Andrew's, Holborn ; John Coleridge Patteson, 1827-1871, Missionary Bishop of Melanesia, whose noble death is recorded on the wayside memorial at Spence Cross; John Taylor Coleridge, 1790-1876, the Judge, of whom it does not become me to speak, and to whose memory friends and neighbours dedicated the beautiful cross in our Churchyard, all these were scholars at the old King's School ; Sir John Kennaway, the father of the present Baronet, upright, scholarly, pious ; Dr. Cornish, Vicar and Schoolmaster, who grew so rooted in the soil of the place, that he became, as it were, its living embodiment ; Thomas Selway, beloved of men, all these and many others I must pass by.

Nor can I do more than simply mention such events as the splitting up of our immense parish into several, the building of our schools, the destruction of the old market-place in the Flexton, and the building of the common-place Town Hall, of the opening of the Cotttage Hospital through the munificence of Mrs. Elliot, of the advent of the Railway.

Time bids me draw to a close. I am not able to bring complete upon the scene events or persons still

SIR JOHN TAYLOR COLERIDGE.

remembered by us. I have rather tried, in all too fragmentary a way to call up the more distant part.

What then of our town to-day? It is different indeed from what it was in former times. Let us not bewail the vanished pomp of Grandisson. It did its work, its day is gone. Of old when travelling was difficult our little town enclosed a little world, self-interested, self-supporting, self-contained. Now the great towns, especially the greatest, London, absorb too much I think of the hopes, the aims,

the ambitions of our folk. I suppose it is in vain to struggle
against the tendency, although we may lament it.

But this much we can do. We can preserve all things
of interest and beauty in the place. We may treasure and
keep green the memory of its worthies. And if our lot
should drive us far from home to seek our fortunes in
other scenes, we may always keep a warm corner in our
heart for the dear old town of Ottery S. Mary.

[FINIS.]